The
TRIPPING
POINT
in
LEADERSHIP

— *Overcoming Organizational Apathy*

David Byrd
Master of Effective Leadership

FOREWORD BY PAUL J. MEYER

The Tripping Point in Leadership — *Overcoming Organizational Apathy*

© 2008 by David Byrd

Published by Pilot Communications Group, Inc.
317 Appaloosa Trail
Waco, TX 76712

ISBN: 978-0-982467-2-5

Printed in the United States of America

HOW TO ORDER:

www.trippingpointbooks.com

Apathy is a natural, human instinct, common to us all, that consistently encourages us to seek a comfort zone in which nothing ever changes.

Dedication

This book is dedicated to all the leaders who have forged the way for the rest of us, and to my mentor and friend, Paul J. Meyer, who demonstrates the characteristics of the effective leader with a consistency and passion to which I have seen no comparison.

Contents

Foreword by Paul J. Meyer

This book is not a cotton candy, pat you on the fanny approach to leadership. Before you finish the first chapter, it will hit you in the gut.

The intent of this book is to wake you up out of your apathy! And not for just an inspirational moment, but for a set of new choices, new direction, and new action for leaders in your company.

For those who don't want to look in the mirror to find out who is there, they should put this book down now. But for you, when you finish and apply the content of this book in your life, you will be an effective leader!

Without any fluff, this very well may be the first leadership book that you can't put down until you finish it!

The first one you will read again and again!

The first one you will underline!

The first one you will choose as a guideline for your future choices and measurement of your effectiveness!

The first one you will want to buy for the leaders in your company!

The first one you will recommend to your peers.

You will be a leader who makes positive choices, has clear vision, attracts the right ideas, has courage to take action, and is known by peers, colleagues, and employees as an effective leader.

David Byrd, master executive and trainer, has nailed it like none other!

Paul J. Meyer
New York Times Best-Selling Author
Founder of SMI, LMI, and 40+ other companies
www.pauljmeyer.com

Introduction

The ebb and flow of life is seemingly random, and there are many circumstances over which none of us have any control, but the ups and downs, losses and gains, and successes and failures of life *are usually directed by certain natural laws*.

Just like gravity, these consistent principles and truths are at the disposal of humankind for its *benefit* or *detriment*.

From the very core of our existence, we were created with certain personal powers that:

A) benefit those of us who **use** them or

B) impede those of us who **ignore** their significance.

This book is written from the perspective of my own life's journey. I have learned from personal and professional experience *that these certain personal powers usually define the qualities of effective leadership*, and effective leaders are needed in all areas of life.

Much has been written on the subject of personal powers, but the purpose of this book is to answer the question:

"Why are these personal powers important to me?"

If we understand the basic reason for our creative design, then those personal powers become much more than a seminar topic. *If we understand* the human flaw for which our personal powers were designed to counteract, then those powers become a pathway to an effective and dynamic lifestyle.

As president of Leadership Management®, Inc., an international training and development company that has over 40 years of experience in helping people develop and use more of their true potential, I came to see just how important effective leadership can be.

> **Effective leadership must be developed. It does not come by chance, position, title, or age.**

I have invested much of my life, over 30 years, in working with top business executives and their organizations. Everyday I hear of "*people problems*" that are presumed to be the cause of ineffectiveness.

Most clients are shocked when they first realize that their people problems are really *symptoms of a natural, human instinct*.

Effective leadership is a unique quality, and I find that it *never just happens*. It is a skill that must be developed, and this development process does not happen naturally in life.

In the absence of this crucial development process, we find young, aspiring leaders:

> **missing significant opportunities to learn and model effective leadership behaviors.**

There are also many current leaders who have already learned from less than effective models, and there are those who have been given decision making authority but have no idea what effective leadership is.

8

Most organizational dysfunction stems from one or all of the above scenarios.

The Tripping Point in Leadership is written as a common-sense guide to enhanced leadership quality. It is not intended to be an exhaustive, academic discourse. ***Its purpose is to serve as a wake up call for aspiring and existing leaders in all walks of life.***

I sincerely hope that these words will create **awareness** among leaders ... and that this **awareness** will result in effective changes in organizations, schools, families, and people around the world.

Effective change begins with **awareness**, and **awareness** always leads to **choice**.

After reading this book, you will be asking the question:

"How will I choose?"

Chapter One

Apathy can trip you up! The first step to overcoming it ... is recognizing it.

Apathy: A Natural, Human Instinct

I had just finished my introductions in front of more than 70 top executives of an international organization when I made a shocking and somewhat risky statement.

I told them that all the organizational problems they had identified on their introductory worksheets were merely symptoms of the same universal problem — **apathy**.

The individual annual incomes of this group ranged from $250,000 to $500,000, *and I had just told them they were apathetic!* At least that is what they heard.

I quickly asked them to withhold their judgment for a moment, and give me a chance to explain before collectively deciding that a high-priced development expert had just insulted them.

As a hush fell over the room, I began to verbally review the general list of people problems that they had provided for me prior to the meeting:

- indecisiveness
- lack of drive
- lack of creativity
- lack of focus
- stagnation
- burnout

11

- imbalance
- the list went on and on.

This was their list, not mine!

I paused for a second and just looked at them. Then I asked each executive to write down the following developmental definition for apathy:

> **A natural, human instinct, common to us all, that consistently encourages us to seek a comfort zone in which nothing ever changes.**

Pens began to move across legal pads. After a few moments, I asked the group this question, **"How many of you know someone in your current organization who is impeded by this description of apathy?"**

The entire group raised their hands in unison.

Then I asked the hard question, **"How many of you have, at some point, suffered from this same description?"**

You could hear a pin drop.

Finally, one person started laughing and courageously raised her hand. Her actions stimulated other colleagues to raise their hands, and the entire room broke into laughter of genuine confession.

Facing the Facts

The word *apathy* is an unfriendly and threatening word to most people, and that is probably the reason I never hear executives use the word to describe problems within their organizations.

Instead, I hear the listing of symptoms, such as:

- burnout
- stagnation
- indecision
- lack of creativity
- lack of motivation
- lack of productivity
- and so on.

These symptoms may sound more professional, academic, clinical, or forgiving, **but symptoms**, if worked on exclusively, **lead an organization on a wild goose chase, fixing symptoms but never solving real problems!**

Comfortable with the Truth

Apathy is a very useful and effective word for me now after years of experience. In fact I have learned that until a person gains an awareness of how the forces of apathy work to impede effectiveness, behavioral change and improvement are out of the question.

Awareness begins with an understanding of apathy as a natural, human instinct common to us all.

Usually when someone is called apathetic, he or she is being accused of indifference. But the working definition I am using for apathy *has little to do with indifference*. It has everything to do with describing the relationship between the basic motivation of security and the natural, human instinct described as apathy.

Take a close look at my working definition of apathy:

> **A natural, human instinct, common to us all, that consistently encourages us to seek a comfort zone in which nothing ever changes.**

Now, ask yourself this question, **"What is one of humankind's basic, motivational drives?"**

According to Maslow's famous book, *A Theory of Human Motivation*, most all human behavior can be traced back to the basic motivation of self-preservation and security. Some may be motivated by higher-level needs, but as soon as their security is threatened, they quickly revert to self-preservation.

> **It is natural for all of us to seek a comfort zone.**

This process of seeking security and building unproductive comfort zones, if left unchecked, leads to behaviors that are usually described as the causes of people problems and ineffectiveness.

In order to demonstrate how the forces of apathy as a natural, human instinct act as the root cause of most individual and organizational dysfunction, I have included the following real case studies, which are typical examples out of hundreds.

(Names have been changed and do not relate to the actual client case.)

14

John, a Senior VP

John is a senior vice president in a large international company. He is 52 years old and has been with the same company for over 27 years.

In talking with John, I asked him this question, **"John, do your employees have any consistent criticism of you or your leadership?"**

He quickly replied, **"Indecision."**

I asked if he believed those critiques to be accurate.

He said, **"I don't think so because with the company in transition now, I have to make sure my decisions are right. It's better not to make a decision at all than to make the wrong one. After all, I'll be retiring in the next few years anyway."**

I interviewed several of John's employees, and what I heard most often was this: **"John is a good man, but he keeps us waiting forever for an answer to our basic requests. His indecision is causing severe delays in production."**

The forces of apathy are the cause of John's problems. Indecision is the *symptom*. John has constructed a comfort zone for himself to avoid the fear of making a bad decision and risking his security.

As a result, his unconscious goal is never to make a mistake. John's comfort zone is a place in which nothing can ever change and mistakes can never happen. John's leadership behavior is unproductive but comfortable.

Ann, a Rising Star

Ann is a young, bright, rising star of one of our clients. She is on a fast track to the top, but she "hit the wall," as she described it.

"I haven't had a new idea in months," she explained. **"I am so exhausted most of the time, I can't even think. My life is nothing but work, and I see no end to it."**

In an interview with Ann's boss, he said, **"Ann has the greatest potential I've ever seen, but her lack of focus on priorities is constantly getting her into trouble. She's got to turn it around because it's affecting her performance."**

Ann's boss sees the symptom of lack of focus while her unproductive behavior is actually a result of the unrecognized forces of apathy.

As unusual as it may seem, Ann finds security in staying busy and overworked. Maintaining the pace of a superhero allows her to never face her insecurities about her competency.

Her overachieving behavior represents a comfort zone in which she can never be threatened by an evaluation of results.

Al, a CEO

Al is the CEO of a small company with 50 employees. Al has had three leadership positions in different companies over the last 10 years. He is 55 years old.

In an initial interview with Al, I asked what he wanted to accomplish with his company in the next 5 to 10 years.

He said, **"What I really want to do is take this company to the next level."**

I quickly asked him to describe this "next level."

He said, **"I want to double revenues to 10 million."**

He beamed with confidence.

My next question caused him some discomfort, **"What obstacles stand in the way of accomplishing this goal?"**

He responded, **"My people."**

I asked him to explain.

> **Symptoms are not the problem. Apathy is the problem.**

"I can't get any buy-in from my leadership team, so I find that it's a lot easier to just do it myself," he went on to say. **"They're good people, but I just can't trust them to get the job done right. If I had some people who would listen to me and do things the way I know how to do them, we could achieve that goal."**

In talking with Al's leadership team, the general consensus is that the team admires Al's work ethic. They want to help, but they feel that he does not trust them to get anything accomplished.

As a result, it is much easier for them to take the support or helper role with Al because he is going to do the job himself anyway.

Al is psychologically secure in his comfort zone. He interprets his lack of belief in people as confident self-reliance.

The problem is that the company will never be able to grow beyond the individual capacities of Al. He is completely unaware of the damage his behavior is causing his company.

The forces of apathy as a natural, human instinct are causing Al to seek a comfort zone in which he never trusts his people. The forces of apathy, not his people, are the cause of Al's poor leadership style.

Jim, a New VP

Jim is a newly promoted VP for a company at which he has been employed over 15 years. He literally rose from the ranks to his current position. He is about 45 years old.

Jim is known for his work ethic and attention to detail. He is a first-class projects person. Completing tasks is his hallmark.

In an interview with Jim, he told me that his greatest frustration is that **"the people problems that fall under my new responsibilities get in the way of my own work. I miss the opportunity to close my door and just complete projects."**

In talking with Jim's boss, I found that Jim is having difficulty assuming his new leadership role. His level of frustration is very noticeable at times, and it is affecting morale.

Completed tasks and projects represent a psychological comfort zone for Jim. His frustrations are not caused by missed opportunities to close his door and complete projects, but the changes that his new job requires is forcing him out of his comfort zone.

What Is the Common Denominator?

The common denominator of every organization in the world is people. Every day people show up for work and bring with them their own unique set of values, beliefs, and behaviors.

Effective leadership development is appropriate for every level of any organization, from the CEO to the stock room clerk. Organizations without a proactive leadership development program at every level of their organization are prime targets for the forces of apathy.

If you were to take any one of those real examples and multiply it by every member of an organization, stagnation and decline would be the only possible result.

Really Taking It to the Next Level

A few years back, I was working with a significant international company in the food services industry. The company had been operational since the 1970s and had grown revenues to a high of over 200 million dollars.

However, when I looked at the company's past, I found that the company had leveled off three years prior and was in the beginning stages of decline.

I immediately began to talk with the leaders about the forces of apathy. They were surprised at my concern and somewhat indignant at the suggestion of apathy.

The CEO said, **"We are debt free with five years of operating capital in the bank. Why should we be concerned with growth? We're doing just fine."**

Remember the developmental definition of apathy:

> **A natural, human instinct, common to us all, that consistently encourages us to seek a comfort zone in which nothing ever changes.**

This company and its leaders were clearly in the beginning stages of apathy with all its declining affects.

Effective leadership development is appropriate for every level of any organization, from the CEO to the stock room clerk.

My first step was to generate a new level of awareness of the available untapped potential existing among the leadership team.

I have learned from experience that behavioral change always begins with awareness, and awareness always leads to choice. **People will always choose to change when they are aware that the change serves their best interest.**

From this new level of awareness among the leadership team, I started a proactive leadership development process for the top leaders. An appropriate level of leadership development was then implemented at every level of the organization.

The company began a new phase of growth within 24 months and has never looked back!

The company discovered that a position of **no growth** is unacceptable, and from this enhanced level of awareness, they counterbalanced the forces of apathy that were threatening their long-term future.

Apathy Is Like Gravity

Apathy, as a natural human instinct, is consistently at work at every level in every organization. The cumulative impact of apathy on an organization is stagnation and ultimate decline.

I have observed that this decline is inevitable unless counterbalanced with a proactive and consistent leadership development program.

Every organization in the world has two things in common:

    1) a present and

    2) a future.

I refer to everything between those two positions as process. Every organization has a process. It may be informal, ineffective, unproductive, or highly productive and effective.

Regardless of the quality of the process, every organization has one. **The quality of the process of the organization determines the quality of the performance of the organization.**

In turn, the quality of the performance of the organization ultimately determines the quality of the future of the organization.

Grow ... Or Decline

Every organization must choose growth. The only alternative to growth is decline. There is no other position for an organization in planning its future.

When an organization's leaders choose growth, that growth must come from enhanced overall performance. That enhanced performance can only come from the development of untapped potential.

Doing more of the same will only deliver similar results. Effective leaders are aware of this vital necessity.

Effective leadership fosters positive and creative work environments, delivers measurable and sustainable results, and maintains the ethical integrity of the workplace.

> **People will always choose to change when they are aware that the change serves their best interest.**

Effective leadership begins with an awareness of how the forces of apathy affect the organization and its people.

Without an awareness of the forces of apathy, people become stuck in ineffective and unproductive comfort zones of their own design, while **ineffective leaders** focus on the symptoms of their people problems.

As a result, one of the most common training and development mistakes I find is where organizations begin designing training programs to fix what has been broken:

a communication seminar to fix ...

communication problems,

a clerical skills seminar to fix ...

a department's lack of focus, or

a policies seminar to fix ...

attention to detail.

Obviously, the problems are never "fixed" because the organizations **are only working on symptoms**, never the real problem.

Apathy, as a natural, human instinct, **is counterbalanced with certain personal powers that were strategically included in our creative, human design.**

> **Change and growth occur when you work to correct the problem, not the symptoms.**

These personal powers are available to everyone, but without some understanding of why these personal powers are important, they are usually ignored as motivational fluff or insignificant soft skills.

Throughout the next four chapters, you will learn about the following personal powers:

1) **choice**,

2) **vision**,

3) **attraction**, and

4) **courage**.

An awareness and understanding of these counterbalancing personal powers can serve as a future foundation for a consistent leadership development model that makes good common sense.

You can **overcome** the negative forces of apathy!

CHAPTER ONE SUMMARY
Points to Remember

1) Most people problems **are usually only symptoms** of the forces of apathy.

2) Apathy is considered **a natural, human instinct that consistently encourages us to seek a comfort zone where nothing can ever change**.

3) Problems **are never fixed** by only working on the symptoms.

4) Humankind's basic motivational drive **is for security**.

5) If left unchecked, the **forces of apathy lead to unproductive and ineffective behaviors**.

6) Apathy, as a natural, human instinct, is **counterbalanced** with certain personal powers **that were strategically included** in our creative, human design.

Chapter Two

Choice represents the potential power to overcome apathy.

The Power of Choice

The power of choice represents one of the most significant resources of humankind. That potential power, however, is governed by a dichotomy.

For example, the cumulative **difference** between a lifetime filled with **good choices** and a lifetime filled with **bad choices** can be dramatic.

There is an old theological joke that explains this dichotomy:

> In one of the first conversations between God and Adam, God said, "Adam since you are the first of my new creation, I have some good news and some bad news. The good news is that I have given you the freedom to choose."
>
> Adam became really excited and said, "That's great! I can do whatever I want!"
>
> God then said, "That leads me to the bad news, Adam. The bad news is that I have given you the freedom to choose."

This joke is a humorous look at a very simple reality: **the gift of choice is a double-edged sword**.

It cuts both ways.

Choices Make or Break You

Our choices can make or break us. We either enjoy the benefits or suffer the consequences of our choices.

Actually, our lives represent the cumulative impact of the choices we make.

The objective of this chapter is for you to:

A) think about choice as a creative power, and

B) consider how that power applies to you and your future as a leader.

I have noticed that effective leaders usually make good choices. Those choices have a cumulative and creative positive impact on the organizations effective leaders serve.

> **I find very smart leaders who are simply not aware of the power of their choices.**

Through experience, I have discovered that **the power of choice is more defined by level of awareness than by level of intelligence**.

I find very smart leaders who are simply not aware of the power of their choices.

The power of choice counterbalances the forces of apathy with a heightened level of awareness regarding the cumulative impact of productive choices.

That awareness consistently pushes you beyond any self-imposed, unproductive comfort zones.

Countless Daily Choices

This is an extreme example, but over the years I have had a practice of speaking to and attempting to befriend some of our nation's homeless. In most of these conversations, I find a total **disconnect** or **denial** of current circumstances as being a result of their bad choices: drugs, alcohol, irresponsibility, etc.

Many of the homeless see themselves as victims of a bad system, and as victims they have no control of their circumstances.

> **Choice paints the color of your emotional space and determines the outline of your future.**

I find that intelligence level has little to do with homelessness. There are some very intelligent people who are homeless. They are simply unaware and give little consideration to the cumulative impact of their choices.

Think about this question:

How many choices do you make everyday?

Fewer than 50?

More than 100?

The reality is that you make 1000s of choices every single day! Moment by moment you choose your perspectives, perceptions, attitudes, and actions.

The journey of life is all about choice. Choice paints the color of your emotional space and determines the outline of your future. The cumulative impact of your life is determined by how you manage the power of choice.

There are three choices that will determine the quality of your future and the effectiveness of your leadership. I would like for you to consider your personal position in relation to these three very important choices.

#1 The Choice of Attitude

What I want you to remember about attitude is that attitude is a choice, not a gimmick. Some resist any discussion of positive attitude.

> **The cumulative impact of your life is determined by how you manage the power of choice.**

They see it as a motivational gimmick, always looking for the good and never being realistic about the bad.

I have even been told that the use of the phrase "positive attitude" is passé and simple-minded as an industry standard. But I have found that attitude is a very important personal choice that determines the quality of your future and the degree of your success.

A good definition of positive attitude is:

> **a predetermined and proactive habit of thought dominated by faith, hope, optimism, and courage.**

The ONLY difference between a positive and negative attitude is personal choice, and the choice of a positive, productive attitude is the most important trait of the effective leader.

In my interviews with effective leaders, the one consistent theme I hear is the power of their positive expectations. *They believe that they generally get out of life what they put into it.*

30

I almost *never find effective leaders who have achieved above their own expectations*. For the sake of humility, I may hear them attempt to downplay their achievements, but at the gut level, they all expected to achieve.

An established attitude of positive expectancy sets the baseline for long-term achievement. You may fall short of your expectations at times, but you *will rarely* achieve above your true expectations.

An attitude is a habit of thought. Your attitudes stem from your basic beliefs about yourself and others and are a result of your consistent thinking process or self-talk.

> **The choice of a positive, productive attitude is the most important trait of the effective leader.**

Of course your thinking process is completely your own personal choice, and effective leaders choose to be driven by positive expectancy. The power of their positive expectations counterbalances the forces of apathy through the expectation of positive outcomes.

Your attitude becomes prophetic of your future and acts as a magnet ... *you actually set up self-fulfilling prophecies regarding your future*. You attract the circumstances that fulfill your expectations.

Negative expectations:

> **fit perfectly into a comfort zone where nothing can change.**

Think of it this way: *If you are expecting something less than the best, a secure comfort zone is a good place to be.*

31

Apathy is a comfortable friend of negative expectations. *Why do you think negative news has a stronger appeal than positive news?*

It is simply because negative news appeals to the forces of apathy as a natural, human instinct and therefore feels more comfortable to many people.

> **Every thought you entertain during the day is either positive or negative.**

> **Your thoughts either energize or drain your vital emotions.**

> **There is no in-between.**

The questions below require some deep self-analysis and soul-searching, but they will help you understand the habits of your thinking. Ask yourself these questions:

- Am I generally **positive** or **negative**?
- Do I expect to **succeed** or **fail**?
- Do I seek to **support** or **criticize**?
- Do I seek to **praise** or **find fault**?
- Do I focus on my **strengths** or seek to hide my **weaknesses**?
- Do I seek to learn from my **mistakes** or be defensive about my **perfection**?
- Do I expect the **best** or the **worst**?
- Do I seek to build others **up** or tear them **down**?
- Do I most often fear **failure** or desire **achievement**?
- Do I seek to **encourage** or **discourage**?

- Do I focus on other people's **strengths** or **weaknesses**?

Find a trusted friend to review your answers to these questions and give him or her freedom to give you honest feedback.

We all have blind spots that are hidden to us ... *but very obvious to others*. You can make great strides of achievement when you confront your blind spots with courage.

> **You attract the circumstances that fulfill your expectations.**

Search for and find ways to change or improve your habits of thought. You must consciously practice positive expectancy. It is not a natural mindset; it requires consistent practice. Leaders rise or fall to the quality of their thinking and expectancy.

The forces of apathy, if left unchecked, consistently drive our attitudes to the secure comfort zone of fear. The emotion of fear is instinctive and serves to protect us, which is a good thing.

However, *many people develop the habit of responding to most circumstances in life from the emotion of fear*. This behavior represents a psychological, secure comfort zone that, unfortunately, leads to negative, unproductive attitudes.

Fearful, negative attitudes pose three significant problems.

1) Fear paralyzes productive actions. The comfort zone of fear leads to negative attitudes which, in turn, get in the way of positive, productive actions.

2) Fear attracts and supports failure. Negative attitudes find comfort in failure. They offer an instant and comfortable excuse to quit or blame something or someone else.

3) Fear eliminates ownership of possible solutions. Negative attitudes destroy creative energy. If something or someone else is responsible for your failure, then possible solutions or lessons learned are beyond your control.

For example seeing yourself as a victim of circumstances may offer some comfort, ***but victims have no control over any possible solutions***. To find solutions, you must be 100% responsible and accountable for your circumstances. Victims have no solutions, but effective leaders must.

The power of choice, in regards to attitude, acts to counterbalance the forces of apathy by developing a healthy, positive perspective of life.

You can control your responses to fear by changing the way you think. ***Attitude is a choice.*** Your attitude can be driven by fear or courage; it is your choice.

To be an effective leader, you have to consistently fight your normal responses to fear because effective leadership demands attitudes that are:

positive,

productive, and

effective.

The first step in attitude development is to make a personal commitment to assume 100% responsibility for your attitudes and behaviors.

The circumstances of life will always be a mix of *good* and *bad*, but your responses to life must always be *positive* and *productive*.

> **The forces of apathy, if left unchecked, consistently drive our attitudes to the secure comfort zone of fear.**

Attitude is truly a choice that holds significant personal power for you.

#2 The Choice of Action

What I want you to remember about action is that action is a choice, not a smokescreen. It is *not how much you do, but the effectiveness of what you do that counts*.

The late Peter Drucker defined effectiveness as:

> **"The process of doing more of what works, abandoning what doesn't, and knowing the difference."**

Sometimes I see people use a great deal of activity as a smokescreen to avoid doing what is most effective. Many top leaders are very busy, but their actions are void of the most critical measure: *effectiveness!*

The only true measure of action is effectiveness because there is no smokescreen within that measure. Effectiveness is a tough task-master. It eliminates all the fluff.

The effective leader consistently chooses effective actions as opposed to comfortable activity.

The forces of apathy consistently encourage us to use our actions as a smokescreen. Think of it this way:

> **If you can look busy and avoid the measure of results, you can psychologically feel secure in your comfort zone of no mistakes and no measurement.**

However, the effective leader uses the *power of choice* by always choosing effective actions. Herein lies the reason effective leaders deliver measurable results:

> **they choose effective actions.**

Effective actions require courage because measurable actions are not always comfortable. The normal human response to uncomfortable or fearful actions is to fill the day with more comfortable activities and avoid the uncomfortable effective actions.

Make a personal commitment to assume 100% responsibility for your attitudes and behaviors.

Instead, make a personal commitment today to *never use comfortable activity as a smokescreen in order to avoid effective actions*. Begin to apply the critical measure of effectiveness to every action you take.

Action is a choice, not a smokescreen. It is not how much you do, but the effectiveness of what you do that counts.

#3 The Choice of Accountability

What I would like for you to remember about accountability is that accountability is a *choice*, not a *crutch*. It pushes you beyond your self-imposed limitations.

In my early years after college, I was a high school football coach and later went on to coach at the college level. I learned one of my most significant leadership lessons while coaching high-potential athletes:

> **Natural talent, such as size, speed, strength, and intelligence, is nothing more than untapped potential, and there is one ingredient required of the gifted athlete in order to develop that potential ... accountability.**

The high-potential athlete must come to accept 100% responsibility for developing and using his or her talents as an effective member of the team.

When a gifted athlete matures to a level of personal accountability, he or she becomes a champion.

You possess an infinite supply of potential! However, to reach that reserve, you must overcome your self-imposed limitations. The very essence of life is the passionate commitment to strive for a better tomorrow.

> **Accountability pushes you beyond your self-imposed limitations.**

If you want to be something tomorrow that you are not today, you need to develop your untapped potential. Doing more of the same will never raise you to another level.

Your untapped potential lies just beyond your comfort zone. Accountability is not comfortable.

> **If you want your life to be filled with abundance and significance, never allow yourself the comfort of an excuse.**

That is probably the reason many top leaders resist tracking their daily activity ... *it holds them account-able to effective actions*.

If you want your life to be filled with abundance and significance, never allow yourself the comfort of an excuse. Accountability eliminates all excuses; accountability is truly a choice, not a crutch.

Regardless of your current accomplishments, you have so much more to give.

Potential represents an endless reserve, and that potential always lies just beyond your comfort zone. Many leaders constantly struggle with their comfort zone.

They straddle two questions:

A) Do I settle for what is?

B) Or do I push toward what could be?

I hope you are asking yourself these questions as well because effective change begins with awareness, ***and awareness always leads to choice***.

You cannot sidestep the issue of choice.

Your choices regarding attitude, action, and accountability will determine the quality of your life and leadership. You must choose, ***so choose wisely***.

CHAPTER TWO SUMMARY
Points to Remember

1) Choice represents a significant resource; **it is a creative, personal power that has a cumulative, positive impact** on the quality of your life.

2) The power of choice is more defined by your level of **awareness** than by your level of **intelligence**. The effective leader is **aware** of the cumulative impact of productive choices.

3) **Attitude is a choice**, not a gimmick. Your attitudes are **prophetic** of your future.

4) Action **is a choice**, not a smokescreen. It is not how much you do but the effectiveness **of what you do that counts**.

5) Accountability **is a choice**, not a crutch. Accountability **pushes you beyond** your self-imposed limitations.

6) Human potential represents an **endless reserve**, and that potential **always lies just beyond your comfort zone**.

Chapter Three

With your power of vision, apathy will be put in its proper place!

The Power of Vision

One of the most distinguishing characteristics of humankind is the creative gift of imagination. We were uniquely created with this ability and were given the faculty of imagination for a purpose.

There is significant, creative power in the ability to imagine your ideal future. This ability is referred to as **vision**.

The effective leader benefits from the power of vision by using his or her imagination to build internal motivations that are stronger than the comfort zone of security.

In other words:

vision counterbalances the forces of apathy by building a picture of the ideal future.

This picture of the ideal future fuels progressive, internal motivations which in turn generate drive and focus.

James Gregory Lord said:

"Vision is more than the future as we imagine it might turn out. It is a willed future … a picture of the future as we want to make it."

The key to a fulfilling, dynamic, and abundant life is vision.

Vision In Action

There were some studies conducted back in the 1960s that scientifically substantiated the power of vision. One of those studies involved a group of behavioral scientists who randomly selected a group of junior high boys and girls and divided them into two groups.

The test:

> **Shoot a basketball through a hoop for a set number of free throws from the foul line on a basketball court.**

The two groups were given an initial test, without any practice, to establish a baseline. Then each group was given one week to practice.

For a set time period each day, the two groups practiced shooting free throws. However, one group **_physically_** practiced with the ball, actually shooting it, while the second group practiced **_mentally_** by imagining themselves standing at the foul line and shooting the ball successfully through the hoop.

After one week of physical versus mental practice, the two groups were pitted against each other in a final test. The purpose was to measure and compare the improvement from the first test.

The results:

> **The test showed that not only did the group who _mentally_ practiced show the highest percentage of improvement, but also they actually beat the group that had practiced with the ball!**

This research was conducted in schools across the nation to establish validity in the findings. The results remained consistent: Using the imagination to mentally practice an ideal, physical performance positively influenced actual results.

From this classic research grew the trend for professional athletes to spend specific practice time on a positive vision of successful performance.

Florence Chadwick

One of my favorite stories demonstrating the power of vision is about Florence Chadwick. On a foggy July 4th morning in 1952, 34-year-old Florence Chadwick waded into the water off Catalina Island, California. *She wanted to become the first woman to swim the Catalina Channel.*

The water was numbingly cold that morning. The fog was dense. Florence could barely see the boats in her own party. Several times sharks approached and had to be driven away. Fatigue had never been her problem. The bone chilling cold was to be her biggest challenge.

More than 15 hours later, she asked to be taken onto one of the boats.

> **Use the power of vision to build internal motivations that are stronger than your comfort zone of security.**

Her trainer told her repeatedly that she was near the shore and urged her not to quit, but when Florence looked toward what should have been the California coastline, all she could see was the dense fog. A few minutes later she succumbed to the icy waters and was taken out of the water. As her body began to thaw, *she discovered that she had quit just half of a mile from the California coast!*

She told a reporter, "I don't want to make excuses, but if I could have seen the shoreline, I would have made it."

Why Clear Vision Is Needed

I have observed that most people will quit just short of their desired outcome if their mind is limited by lack of vision.

I have also observed that lack of vision will cause top leaders to experience **burnout** and **stagnation**.

> **Without vision, organizations become disorganized, inefficient, ineffective, and filled with fear.**
>
> **Without vision, people quit.**
>
> **Without vision, people perish.**

Clear vision is the key to a full, dynamic, and abundant future.

Ask yourself these questions:

- What vision do I hold for my future?
- How much time do I spend imagining my future as I want it to be?
- How clearly and vividly do I see my future?
- How do I feel when I take time to think about my future?

If you can answer these questions with clarity, **you are using the power of vision as an advantage over the forces of apathy**.

If, however, you have difficulty with these questions, at least *you are now aware* of the significant importance of vision, and effective change always begins with awareness.

> **Most people will quit just short of their desired outcome ... if their mind is limited by lack of vision.**

What Is Vision?

After years of presentations and ensuing discussions on vision, I have come to understand that there are many misconceptions about what vision is.

Many believe:

> **that any discussion of vision is an idle waste of time and entertain the discussion only as an eloquent afterthought.**

The conventional thinkers of any group:

> **would much rather iron out the details first before drifting off on some lofty cloud.**

Many people say:

> **that they just do not have time during the day to spend imagining something that may not happen.**

However, ***vision is one of the fundamental powers of the effective leader***. It is a quality that makes the effective leader unique.

The most difficult task in planning is designing and building a passionate vision:

> **a willed future,**

> **a picture of the future,**

> **as you want to make it.**

Without a driving, inspirational vision, planning is reduced to nothing more than an uninspired to-do list. **Vision places the compelling why behind what you do.**

Why Vision Produces Resistance

There are two reasons why the issue of vision produces such resistance.

> **#1 — Past conditioning.** How many times have you heard someone reprimanded for daydreaming instead of doing? As a result, you negatively associate vision with a waste of time.

| **Effective change always begins with awareness.** | The power of vision involves your imagination, but it should never be associated with childish daydreaming or wasting time. |

> **#2 — Fear.** How many times have you dreamt of something that never came to pass? As a result, you

negatively associate vision with something that is probably not going to happen, so you naturally avoid any discussion of vision out of fear of risk.

Fear limits your ability to build clear vision **because you are afraid of committing to something that may not happen**.

I have dealt with resistance to vision both personally and organizationally. From those experiences, I have developed a system for building clear vision.

> **Vision places the compelling why behind what you do.**

I suggest the following five step system to enhance your use of the power of vision.

Step #1 — Start and Keep an Ongoing Dream List

A dream list is simply a list of wishful goals that you have always wanted to accomplish ... everything that you have ever ...

wanted to be,

wanted to have, or

wanted to do.

Take off the judge's robe and let your imagination run free. This exercise forces you to use your imagination. Dreams are the fuel for our internal drive.

I have kept a dream list updated annually since 1979. Some might think this a silly undertaking, but I have learned from this exercise that we attract to ourselves that which we set out for ourselves. What we see is what we get.

Step #2 — Write a Vision Statement

The statement should be written in paragraph format and should be no more than one page. It should be dated five to 10 years into the future, but written in present tense.

Write a clear description of your ideal future, as if you are already there.

You should be somewhat realistic, but be careful not to limit your potential. This description should express your *heart* and *soul*.

Step #3 — Set Annual Goals

Your annual goals should move you closer to your vision and your goals should always be driven from vision.

Each year review your dream list and set specific, measurable goals. Ask yourself:

> **What can I realistically accomplish this year that will move me closer to my vision?**

This is where specific goals begin to bring you closer to your vision. Each goal should be:

- specific,
- measurable,
- attainable,

- realistic,
- tangible, and
- include a target date for completion.

I recommend that you work with no more than three to five annual goals.

Step #4 — Review Your Vision Statement

Review your vision statement annually and make revisions. Your evaluation should always be about how compelling the vision is, *never how realistic it is*.

Vision is never about reality. **Vision is always about using the gift of imagination to visualize your ideal future.**

That compelling vision then drives your daily actions and behaviors.

> **Take off the judge's robe and let your imagination run free!**

Step #5 — Share Your Vision Statement

With a mentor, share your vision statement, and ask him or her to hold you accountable. *Accountability* and *results management* are two of the strongest motivations I have ever experienced.

For example I can maintain my physical conditioning or raise it to a higher level much more effectively if I have a trainer. Why? Because the trainer pushes me to a higher level and holds me accountable for my goals.

Many people are afraid of accountability because it requires commitment. ***Commitment puts the reality of your vision on the line.*** If you resist accountability for your commitments, you trade the drive of an inspiring vision for the fear of commitment.

Vision is never about reality.

Effective leaders are aware of how the power of vision counterbalances the forces of apathy.

Burnout, stagnation, lack of focus, and **lack of drive** are merely *symptoms* of the forces of apathy and are inevitable without a passionate vision.

The power of vision keeps the effective leader *moving toward* a passionate vision for tomorrow, rather than settling into a comfort zone of security today.

Florence Chadwick ... Continued

I left you hanging with the Florence Chadwick story. Two months later, she swam the Catalina Channel.

This time she made sure it was a clear day because she had learned that she must be able to see her goal. Not only did she become the first woman to swim the Catalina Channel, she also beat the men's record time by two hours!

Florence discovered what all effective leaders already know:

What you see is what you get!

CHAPTER THREE SUMMARY
Points to Remember

1) The **creative power of imagination** is unique to humankind.

2) The power of vision **builds internal motivations** that **are stronger** than any comfort zone of security.

3) Vision **is the fuel** for the fires of positive expectancy.

4) Many people will quit **just short of their desired outcome** if their minds are **limited** by lack of vision.

5) Vision places **the compelling why** behind what you do.

6) **You may resist the use of vision** because of past conditioning and/or fear.

7) You can **use** the five step system to **build** clear vision.

8) What you see **is what you get!**

Chapter Four

Use your power of attraction to step over every form of apathy.

The Power of Attraction

Have you ever known someone who always seemed to boost your energy or just made you feel better when he or she was around?

In contrast, have you ever known someone who seemed to drain your energy or someone whom you were always trying to avoid?

This is an example of the *positive* and *negative* forces of attraction at work.

Remember this:

> **The impact you have as a leader in the lives of other people will be determined by how you develop and use the power of attraction.**

An Unexpected Effective Leader

In 1993 a hunched-over, elderly, seemingly fragile, little woman was at the center of attention at the National Prayer Breakfast in Washington, D.C. She was there by invitation to address some of America's top leaders.

Her words were flavored with love and seasoned with truth. She was complimentary, challenging, and a little critical.

Those of the political scene are not usually accustomed to inviting criticism, but everyone was attuned to her carefully selected words. This little woman was the leader of over 500 missions in 100 countries.

- She had no personal possessions but commanded the resources of millions of dollars.
- She had no power other than what was willingly given to her.
- Her power was attractive because it was genuine and not manipulative.
- She only wanted the common good.

This is a short description of the attractive power of **Nobel Peace Prize winner Mother Teresa**.

What Effective Leaders Do

The life demonstrated by Mother Teresa is a good working example of effective leadership. Effective leadership is not a manipulative façade by a charismatic personality.

Quite often, the power of attraction can and is used by people for their own self-interest. In contrast, the effective leader uses the power of attraction to counterbalance the forces of apathy by avoiding the secure comfort zone of self-centeredness.

To better understand the power of attraction, try this exercise:

> **Think of someone you know, like, and trust. Now ask yourself this question, "What makes me feel this way about that person?"**

As you list the actions, characteristics, and traits of the person you know, like, and trust, **you are describing the very ingredients of the power of attraction**.

I must admit that some people are born with a natural attractiveness, and other people really have to work at it. But regardless of your inheritance, you can develop the power of attraction.

I am not inferring a manipulative, polished façade to hide behind. In fact manipulation **plays no part** in the genuine power of attraction.

I have discovered through experience that there are five absolutes that form the foundation for the power of attraction.

#1 — Focus On Others First

The story of Mother Teresa demonstrates this distinction. **Effective leaders always deliver measurable results by developing the strengths of those around them.**

This leadership style **is not to be confused with the comforter model of leadership** where the leader simply feels compassion for all people and therefore does all their work for them.

> **Effective leadership is not a manipulative façade by a charismatic personality.**

Rather, the **effective leader demands the best from people by building on their strengths rather than focusing on their weaknesses.**

The effective leader is always an encourager. His or her first consideration regarding a decision is this:

How will this decision best benefit those involved?

Focusing on others first **does not mean** that you disregard your own best interest. Self-interest is always a vital part of the equation, but never first.

Self-centeredness comes from the habit of always considering self first. The forces of apathy are at play here.

Self-preservation, which is a basic, human motivation, **leads to self-centeredness which, in turn, represents the security of a psychological comfort zone**.

Focusing first on your own self-interest leads to dysfunctional, egotistical behavior.

This behavior is very prevalent, unfortunately, but not very attractive.

The power of attraction is attractive **because it is genuine and can be trusted**.

The effective leader focuses on others first and, as a result, attracts

buy-in,

cooperation, and

commitment!

#2 — Commitment and Resolve Are Consistently Attractive

A very important ingredient in the power of attraction is being goal-directed. *People are not attracted to aimless drifters.* None of us would be attracted to a person who had no idea of his or her direction, commitment, or resolve.

An attitude of I'*m-just-trying-this-out-for-awhile-to-see-if-it will-work* **is not attractive**, and others can read that non-commitment like a book.

The power of attraction:

> **is built on clear direction, firm commitment, and resolve.**

You may be fearful, uncertain, and insecure, but if you have the resolve to do what it takes for as long as it takes, you will succeed.

Others will see that resolve and be attracted to it.

After I had finished the leadership development work with my very first client back in 1979, he told me why he had decided to hire me to work with his company.

He said, "I wanted a touch of the passion I felt from you about effective leadership."

This was the first time I recognized how the power of attraction really works.

Passion, *commitment*, and *resolve* are key ingredients in the power of attraction, and those qualities come from being a *sold-out*, *committed*, *goal-directed* person.

#3 — A Positive Self-Image Is Worth More Than Gold

You cannot hide your true self-image. A positive self-image counterbalances the natural forces of apathy by never allowing self-doubt to become a comfort zone of security.

You can test your self-image as positive or negative *by simply listening to your self-talk*.

> **Are you confirming your success or your failure?**

We all talk to ourselves, some verbally and some silently, but nonetheless, we are in constant conversation with ourselves, moment by moment.

Listen to what you say to yourself everyday, and ask yourself these questions:

A) Am I confirming my success or my failure?

B) Am I confirming my positive self-image or my feelings of self-doubt?

Some may be surprised by this confession, but I have to fight fearful thoughts everyday. *I believe everyone does.*

Every time a fearful thought comes to mind ...

I intentionally

replace it

with a positive affirmation of faith.

I once heard a very wise saying that went like this:

Fear knocked at the door of my mind; faith answered the door and found no one there.

That is my affirmation for every fearful thought. Repeating positive affirmations to yourself builds your positive self-image, and a positive self-image is attractive.

Everyone wants to associate with a person who is:

> **Pessimism is the opposite of positive expectancy.**

- courageous

- honest

- compassionate

- encouraging

Only a person **with a positive self-image** can possess such qualities.

#4 — You Must Be Aware Of and Attentive to How Other People See You

Your first impression is probably the most important, but your **consistent impressions** have a cumulative impact that either attract or repel.

I read a book back in the mid-seventies entitled *Dress for Success*. One of the most important lessons I learned from that book was how important the little things are to other people.

For instance, did you know that the first thing most people physically notice about you is your shoes?

I know this seems shallow, *but I have learned that it is important to know how other people see you and to evaluate their impressions*.

So I decided that if most people are going to form a first impression based on my shoes, I will make sure my shoes look good.

Some people say:

What does it matter how I look?

Who I am is more important.

I agree, but the effective leader understands that good impressions enhance his or her favorable impressions.

We live in a physical environment, and we attract or repel by the impressions we give.

Those cumulative impressions are formed by others from the observations of the little things, such as well-groomed fingernails and hair, clean, freshly pressed clothes, encouraging attitudes, timeliness, and follow through.

You may not like doing these things, but you cannot argue with the facts. If you are serious about developing the power of attraction, pay close attention to:

- how you dress,

- act, and

- present yourself.

With that said about physical impressions, I cannot leave this issue without mentioning the most unfavorable and negative impression you can make ... *the impression of pessimism*.

Pessimism repels faster than any other negative impression you can make.

However, regardless of the obvious negative impact of pessimism, I see it almost everyday.

> **Focusing on others first does not mean that you disregard your own best interest ... self-interest is always a vital part of the equation, but never first.**

Pessimism is the opposite of positive expectancy.

There is no power in pessimism. It is an energy drain for an individual or an organization.

Here is the real question:

> **If there is so much negative associated with the mindset of pessimism, why is it so prevalent?**

The answer?

> **The natural forces of apathy.**

If optimism is the language of effectiveness, then pessimism is the language of apathy.

Pessimism speaks of no change:

let's keep everything like it is ...

even if it doesn't work ...

we tried that before ...

impossible ...

yes, but ...

Does this language sound familiar? The comfort zone of apathy is comfortable because nothing is expected to change.

| First impressions and consistent impressions. Both are vitally important. |

Positive expectancy is attractive; pessimism is unattractive. You must adopt the language of positive expectancy if you desire the power of attraction.

#5 — Confidence Is the Most Attractive Impression You Can Make

Confidence always attracts positive outcomes. Now here is the catch when it comes to confidence:

You build confidence from successful attempts.

In other words, you try something, it works, and you now have more confidence for the next attempt.

However, if you have just started something new or restarted something and have had zero successful attempts, your first, human reaction is to quit or blame something or someone else. It is a natural, human response.

The most important lesson to learn in being an effective leader is that **no one has ever accomplished great things by quitting**, and when you are in a leadership position, **there is no one else to blame**.

What do you do then?

Find a proven system and stick with it until you begin to experience successful attempts. Stop wasting negative energy on reinventing the wheel.

If you do not have a proven system, find someone with experience, and ask them to help you build one.

> **You may be fearful, uncertain, and insecure, but if you have the resolve to do what it takes for as long as it takes, you will succeed.**

Consistency within a proven system will beat creative brilliance 90% of the time.

Getting the Power of Attraction Into You

The foundation for the power of attraction is:

- considering others first,
- being goal-directed,
- having a positive self-image,
- making good impressions, and
- developing confidence.

The power of attraction is most important in influencing others, and it should always be genuine.

No one has ever accomplished great things by quitting.

I have heard the quote, "Fake it until you make it," but I resist the shallow message of that affirmation.

I prefer this affirmation:

"I am sure of what I hope for and certain of what I do not see!"

This is the very definition of faith. This affirmation of faith, when lived out, *is interpreted by others* as courage, and courage is always attractive.

CHAPTER FOUR SUMMARY
Points to Remember

1) The effective leader **never uses** a charismatic façade to manipulate others.

2) The effective leader **uses the power** of **attraction** to counterbalance the forces of apathy by **avoiding the secure comfort zone of self-centeredness**.

3) When you describe the characteristics of people you know, like, and trust, **you are describing the ingredients of the power of attraction**.

4) The habit of **focusing on your own self-interest** first leads to dysfunctional, egotistical behavior.

5) The effective leader **focuses on others first** and, as a result, attracts **buy-in, cooperation**, and **commitment**.

6) Commitment, resolve, and confidence **are consistently attractive**.

7) A **positive self-image** counterbalances the forces of apathy by never allowing self-doubt to become a comfort zone.

8) **Everyone wants to associate** with a person who is courageous, honest, compassionate, and encouraging.

Chapter Five

It takes courage to overcome apathy,
courage that anyone can develop.

The Power of Courage

Awareness of the negative impact from the forces of apathy within an organization *is a critical issue for all leaders*.

In the last three chapters of this book, we have examined how the creative powers of choice, vision, and attraction serve *to counterbalance* the forces of apathy within an organization and its leaders.

It seems only appropriate to save the most critical, creative power for last:

the power of courage!

Courage comes in different packages. There is *physical courage* that is demonstrated, for example, by our armed forces personnel.

There is also *intellectual courage* exhibited by thought-provoking writers who challenge us to look at issues from different positions.

The most important type of courage to a leader is *emotional courage*.

Personal success will always be just beyond the grasp of those who do not develop the power of emotional courage.

Emotional Courage Is What?

Just what is emotional courage? It is and accomplishes a lot more than most people can imagine. Consider this:

Emotional courage *picks you up when you fail*.

Emotional courage *keeps you acting on your goals* regardless of circumstances or what other people say, think, or do.

Emotional courage *brings stability and security* to your business and home.

Emotional courage *takes calculated risks*.

Emotional courage *is the fuel for the fires* of positive expectancy.

Emotional courage *dares to dream*.

Emotional courage *is contagious*.

Emotional courage *stands tall with optimism* when everyone else is losing theirs.

Emotional courage *faces its blind spot* and says, "I can improve."

Emotional courage *faces fears with an I-will-win attitude*.

Emotional courage *never wastes time* placing blame because it sustains itself with personal accountability.

These passionate statements demonstrate why I believe emotional courage to be the most important personal power of the effective leader.

What Is Your Level of Emotional Courage?

On a scale of 1 to 7, with 1 being the lowest and 7 being the highest, mentally rank your **personal** level of emotional courage.

Here is the reality of this measurement for any leader:

Anything below a 6 is in the danger zone.

The interesting thing about emotional courage is that there is no in-between position. *You either have it or you do not.*

If you ranked yourself a 6 or 7, you have more than enough emotional courage to weather any storm that comes your way.

> **Personal success will always be just beyond the grasp of those who do not develop the power of emotional courage.**

However, if you ranked yourself a 5 or less, I have some good news:

> **You can develop the power of emotional courage.**

In fact the only way to get it is to develop it. *We do not naturally possess this quality.* None of us were born with the quality of emotional courage.

How to Develop Emotional Courage

A good starting point for developing emotional courage is an understanding of what it is:

Emotional courage is your personal, conditioned capacity to respond with positive actions rather than negative beliefs to all life events.

I have a very good friend who lost almost every personal, financial asset in the economic down-turn of the late 70s. He was in the construction business, building residential housing, when the short-term interest rates soared to over 20% overnight.

> **No one is born with emotional courage. Everyone must develop it.**

With his bankers jumping ship, *he had no choice but to get out of that business and start anew*. He chose a new industry in a new location. The move was difficult for him and his family, but my friend responded with positive actions rather than negative beliefs about himself or his future.

Today my friend is heading up a very significant international company.

We are born with neither bravery nor cowardice. *Both of these responses to life events are conditioned responses.* Everyone must confront doubt and fear.

Those leaders with the developed capacity of emotional courage respond to doubt and fear *with positive actions* rather than negative beliefs.

70

To develop emotional courage, you must **redirect your thinking** and **alter your attitude** about yourself and your circumstances. I suggest following four steps to develop emotional courage.

#1 — Believe In Your Potential

It is difficult to be courageous when you do not believe in yourself. Your current capacities and abilities may not be sufficient to address your current circumstance or situation, but you have the untapped potential to handle any circumstance or situation.

You simply have to take positive action to develop that potential. The alternative is to settle into a comfort zone of negative belief.

> **Develop your potential ... or settle into a comfort zone. Those are the ONLY two options we have.**

Symptoms of negative beliefs include:

> *doubt*,

> *procrastination*,

> *indecisiveness*, and

> *pessimism*.

An outside-in perspective can help here. People around you see potential in you that you may not see.

Make a list of your top five personal strengths, starting with the greatest strength.

Then find a trusted friend or mentor to review your list and confirm or add to it.

As an effective leader, you should **build on your strengths** rather than focus on your weaknesses. The degree of your success and achievement in life is determined by how well you develop your potential and use your strengths.

Your weaknesses:

> *simply become dangers to be avoided!*

#2 — Develop a Healthy Attitude Toward Mistakes, Failures, and Negative Outcomes

You will spend much of your life dealing with negative outcomes. Negative outcomes, mistakes, and failures often throw the average person for a loop.

Exercise your power of choice!	However, in the real world of life, it is common to make mistakes and actually fail, and there will *always* be negative circumstances over which you may not have any control. The reality is any of us can fail.

I find it interesting that most very successful people have failed more than the average person.

Failing at something is a common event, but **seeing yourself as a failure** comes from your past conditioning of fear and insecurity. Your circumstances never define who you are ... **your actions do**.

Responding to life with habitual, critical, and pessimistic attitudes *is a reflection of your internal fears*. You truly are what you believe yourself to be. Your behaviors and actions demonstrate your beliefs.

If you are filled with:

fear,

worry, and

doubt ...

your behaviors demonstrate that!

If you are:

goal-directed and

filled with optimism and

faith ...

your behaviors demonstrate that as well!

Behaviors demonstrate your *TRUE beliefs about yourself and others.*

To develop emotional courage, you must start with a healthy attitude toward all life events, the good and the bad.

> **Respond to doubt and fear with positive actions rather than negative beliefs.**

The smallest beginnings are better than the greatest intentions, so get started by writing a statement describing how you will positively respond to the next negative outcome.

You cannot control all the circumstances of life, but **you must control your responses to those circumstances**.

Emotional courage to the effective leader is a predetermined, productive mindset toward negative events and circumstances.

#3 — Break Out of Your Negative Past Conditioning By Exercising Your Power of Choice

I talk with people everyday who seem to be trapped in self-fulfilling prophecy of their own design. They experience:

> *failure*,

> *procrastination*,

> *indecisiveness*, and

> *fear*.

Our past conditioning sometimes leads us in undesirable directions. **We can change that by exercising our power of choice.** We have the freedom to choose our responses to life.

> **Failing at something is a common event, but seeing yourself as a failure comes from your past conditioning of fear and insecurity.**

Our thoughts are simply choices that design our futures, and we are 100% in control of those thoughts.

Thoughts lead to habits, and habits lead to behaviors.

To develop emotional courage, you must break out of your current conditioning by consciously choosing to act courageously.

It is within every person's power to choose!

#4 — Redesign Your Attitudes by Displacement

Everyone has some fear of failure. Unfortunately, the fear of failure usually leads to negative attitudes and behaviors.

The fear of failure causes you to **protect yourself** by blaming or procrastinating. You psychologically rationalize saying:

> **"If it is never my fault, or if I never get started, I can never fail."**

This unproductive behavior is called rationalization. Rationalization causes you to think that *if you never play* the game, you *will never lose*.

This rationalization, however, causes you never to try, which is obviously self-defeating. To develop emotional courage, *you must displace rationalization*.

> **Learn to displace your thoughts of rationalization with productive thoughts of emotional courage.**

The theory of displacement says that:

> **you can exchange your thoughts of rationalization for productive thoughts of emotional courage.**

It is like replacing dirty water in a glass by continuously filling the glass with clean, fresh water. The new displaces the old.

Consciously practice this process by ***displacing*** every negative rationalization with ***fresh, positive thoughts*** of courage.

Developing emotional courage is not easy, but it is a necessary journey for the effective leader.

CHAPTER FIVE SUMMARY
Points to Remember

1) Personal success **will always be just beyond the grasp** of those who do not develop the power of emotional courage.

2) The interesting thing about emotional courage is that **you either have it or you do not have it**; there is no in-between.

3) The power of emotional courage **must be developed**; you **do not naturally** possess this quality.

4) Emotional courage is **your personal, conditioned capacity** to respond to all life events with positive actions rather than negative beliefs.

5) We are born with **neither bravery nor cowardice**; both of these are conditioned responses.

6) **Follow the four steps** to develop emotional courage.

Chapter Six

Apathy is no match for the effective leader!

The Effective Leader

Appointed leaders fill the halls and offices of every organization in the world. However, being *delegated* the role of leader *does not automatically qualify* someone as an effective leader.

Effective leaders are unique.

They are **consistent**.

They know **what works**.

They know **what does not work**.

As a result, they foster positive and creative work environments, deliver measurable and sustainable results, and maintain the ethical integrity of the workplace.

Appointed Leaders Need a Development Process

Every appointed leader **needs a proven and consistent leadership development process** to hone his or her effective leadership skills.

I mean no slight, but appointed does not equal qualified. The *only* true measure of leadership quality is:

effectiveness.

79

Effectiveness is a constant process of multiplying what works and eliminating what does not. Effective leaders are aware of their personal, creative powers and **how the forces of apathy** affect people and the organization.

The 6 Qualities of an Effective Leader

I have found over the years, from experience and from study[1], that it would take more pages than anyone would read to completely discuss all the assessments and qualifying characteristics of the effective leader.

> **The only true measure of leadership quality is effectiveness.**

The goal here is to simply generate awareness among existing and future leaders as to the significance of effective leadership. And as you know, **all change must first begin with awareness.**

With that said, here are the 6 qualities of the effective leader:

#1 — Effective Leaders Believe in People

One of the dramatic qualities of the effective leader is the skill of **developing people**. This skill comes from the effective leader's high belief and expectations.

It is rare that I find a person who possesses this skill naturally or to perfection. This is truly a skill that must be **developed** and consciously **practiced**.

The values of effective leaders demonstrate their belief in people. Effective leaders *value the potential of all people* and expect everyone under their charge to be responsible and effective.

This *positive expectation* of and high belief in people builds a positive *self-fulfilling prophecy*.

In other words:

Effective leaders usually get what they expect!

Positive beliefs about people support effective leadership behaviors, while negative beliefs about people support less than effective leadership behaviors.

High expectations and belief in people are the key characteristics of the effective leader.

> **The skill of developing people ... must be practiced.**

#2 — Effective Leaders Attract Employee Involvement

One of the most common terms I hear in working with organizational leaders is "*buy-in*."

They talk about first gaining buy-in from their **leadership team**, then from their **level managers**, and then from the **entire organization**.

Sadly, six months later I hear:

> "Well, we couldn't get the project off the ground because we couldn't get the *buy-in* from our people."

Some years ago, a *Wall Street Journal* study discovered that of all the strategic initiatives undertaken by the organizations in the study, **approximately 80%** of the initiatives failed within the **first year**.

Something is not working!

There is an old saying:

> **The fish stinks from the head down.**

And this is what I believe that means:

> **Leadership must take full responsibility for these less-than-impressive results.**

Instead of **seeking** buy-in, effective leaders **attract** it. They attract buy-in by expanding the involvement of everyone under their charge.

People always buy into things for which they are **involved in creating** and for which they are **delegated responsibility**. Expanded involvement promotes collaboration, which, in turn, enhances decision quality.

The effective leader is aware of this vital issue of expanded involvement.

#3 — Effective Leaders Communicate Effectively

Communication is a two-way street: There is always a giver and a receiver. The communication **given** and the understanding **received** must be congruent and unimpeded, or effective communication has not taken place.

Often when leaders are describing communication problems within their organizations, I find that those problems are usually stimulated *from the top down*. That is because organizations usually model the communication styles of their leaders.

Again, leadership

  must assume

  the *responsibility*

  for *establishing*

  the *proper environment*

  for *effective*

  communication.

Most often the problem is that the leaders *are not aware* of the components of effective communication.

Effective communication is all about style. We all have a certain style of communicating. This style is usually learned by **past experience** and **conditioning**. Your style may be effective or ineffective.

> **Effective leaders don't seek *buy-in* ... they attract it.**

Interestingly, I find that those leaders with the most ineffective communication style *usually think of themselves as good communicators*. Therein lies the problem.

Effective leaders *are aware* of the importance of both feedback and exposure in their communication style.

Have you ever worked with someone who constantly asked you questions but never exposed any information about how or why your answers were important?

> **Leaders with the most ineffective communication style usually think of themselves as good communicators.**

It is frustrating!

This is an example of an overuse of feedback seeking and not enough exposure.

On the other hand, have you ever worked with people who could not stop talking about themselves?

That is frustrating AND annoying!

This is an obvious misuse of exposure in the absence of sufficient feedback seeking.

There are two fundamental steps in developing an effective communication style:

> **FIRST — become aware of your existing communication style.**

> **SECOND — learn what an effective communication style looks like.**

With this awareness, a gap between your current style and the effective communication model ***is established***.

This gap defines the development process needed to move from your current communication style to a more effective style of communication. This is an effective development process for improved communications.

I have observed **complete** and **positive** culture changes within organizations when leaders assume the responsibility for establishing an effective communication environment.

#4 — Effective Leaders Use Real Motivators

I find it interesting that most leaders do not know what really motivates people.

- Some leaders use **fear**.
- Some use **incentives**.
- Some use a **combination of both**.

Any of these forms of motivation is the "***carrot and stick***" approach.

The problem with the "carrot and stick" approach is that:

1) today's "carrot" incentive *always* becomes tomorrow's **expected benefit**, and

2) the "stick" *only works* when the fearful leader with the stick **is present**.

> **Leaders become aware, then they take action to change.**

The only form of permanent, self-sustaining motivation is personal motivation.

People act instinctively from their own internal motivations. We may acquiesce to the temporary force of external motivation, but only for a short time.

The effective leader *is aware of how to use the personal, internal motivations of people in support of the common good of the organization*.

Everyone is first motivated by the basic needs for security, but once those basic needs are met, people move to higher-level needs, such as:

- belonging,
- being respected,
- being trusted, and
- being given responsibility.

A few years ago, *USA Today* surveyed people asking what they wanted from a job. The results of the survey showed that the incentive of more money *fell far behind* these higher level motivators as the source of true job satisfaction.

> # The only form of permanent, self-sustaining motivation is personal motivation.

Every leader should learn as much as they possibly can about how personal, internal motivation can passionately drive unimaginable results.

#5 — Effective Leaders Know How to Share Power

The true issue of power is not about its use or misuse. Rather, it is the *sharing of power* that is the real issue. The effective leader exercises power appropriately by sharing it.

The following examples demonstrate the differences of **using power** versus **sharing power**.

Janet, Senior VP of Company A:

Very much in control in her position as senior vice president of her company, Janet is detail oriented and almost consumed with perfection. She believes that she is incapable of mistakes.

Control is very important to her; she must have control of every project assigned to her department. The power to exercise that control is hers and hers alone. Her staff waits for instructions daily.

No one would dare operate outside those instructions.

> **Effective leaders exercise power appropriately ... by sharing it.**

She is a tough task master. Through her use of power she gets the job done, or blame is quickly assigned elsewhere.

When she must travel, not much is accomplished in her absence because the power of her position goes wherever she goes.

She has been assigned the power of the position, and she uses it with complete control.

This is obviously an extreme example of the misuse of power, but as extreme as it is, I have observed *many* leaders just like Janet.

Audrey, Senior VP of Company B:

Rising from the ranks to her position as senior vice president of her company, Audrey is a strong leader with strong opinions. Those opinions tend to dominate meetings, so she has learned to keep her opinions to herself in order to provide opportunities for feedback from her staff. She has found that if her opinions get on the table first, they tend to bias the staff, and new ideas are stifled.

CEOs need effective leaders.

Audrey is always encouraging creative thought from her staff, so she always gives her people the freedom to make common-sense judgments regarding routine operations.

Because she also travels, she has developed a #1 and #2 person and assigned them responsibility for operations when she is absent.

She believes that mistakes are the path to more effective operations, so mistakes are treated as learning experiences. She tells her people, **"Mistakes are okay as long as we learn how not to make the same mistakes again."**

She is being considered for another promotion because her department runs so effectively. Her staff takes pride in how well the department runs. Everyone in that department feels that they share the success of the team.

This too is obviously an extreme example of the sharing of power rather than the use of power, but I believe every CEO would say that Audrey would be a better hire than Janet.

And you know every employee would rather work for an effective leader!

Why would CEOs want a leader like Audrey in their company? Without question, it is because she is an effective leader!

#6 — Effective Leaders Use the Most Effective Style of Leadership

There are five different styles of leadership:

1) the **Comforter**,

2) the **Regulator**,

3) the **Task Master**,

4) the **Manipulator**, and

5) the **Developer**.

Statistical research[1], done by Jay Hall, Ph.D., University of Texas, concluded which style is most effective:

5) the Comforter was the *least effective*,

4) the Regulator was *next to last* in effectiveness,

3) the Task Master was *moderately* effective,

2) the Manipulator *more* effective, and

1) the Developer was the *most effective* style.

The most amazing result of the research is that the Developer style was determined to be:

92% *effective* in the execution of the characteristics of the effective leader mentioned above!

Employees want effective leaders.

The closest style was a distant second with a 55% effectiveness rate.

The Developer is almost *twice as effective* as any other leadership style!

That is because the Developer demonstrates all of the effective leadership qualities:

- **believes in people,**
- **attracts involvement,**
- **is an effective communicator,**
- **uses internal, personal motivation,**
- **shares the power,** and
- **practices the most effective style of leadership.**

Effective Leadership Is a Choice

Many leaders will choose to deny their need to change anything. Some will hold onto conditioning from past models, and some will worry that they will be taken advantage of if they trust people.

> **I find leaders who have sold-out to a compassionate, caring model of leadership, but it is merely a reflection of their mistrust of people.**

In addition, much has been written recently about servant leadership.

That input has simply *confused* the entire issue. I find leaders who have sold-out to a compassionate, caring model of leadership, but it is merely a reflection of their mistrust of people.

These leaders have **such a low belief in people** that they protect, isolate, and do the work for them.

They see people as **being needy** because they are incapable of effective performance.
This is not servant leadership!

If you truly aspire to servant leadership, you must:

> **believe in**,

>> **trust**,

>>> **empower**,

>>>> **challenge**, and

>>>>> **develop**

your people. If you truly love your people, you will demand their best, not coddle and protect them.

Regardless of all the books that have been written about servant leadership, regardless of your theology or beliefs, the real servant leader is the **Developer** — the effective leader.

> **If you truly love your people, you will demand their best, not coddle and protect them.**

Effective leaders are never concerned with "style flexing."

> **They have learned a statistically proven model of leadership.**

Effective leaders never have to question which style to use.

They simply compare their intended actions to the model of the Developer.

Anyone of sound mind can learn the Developer leadership style and become an effective leader.

---

[1]In 2002, Leadership Management®, Inc. acquired the exclusive license agreement for the tools and assessments of Teleometrics™ International. All of these tools and assessments were developed from the statistically validated research of Jay Hall, Ph.D., University of Texas. This research was reported in his classic The Achieving Manager study found in his book *Models for Management: The Structure of Competence*. This is one of the largest bodies of research ever compiled in the field of leadership/management development.

CHAPTER SIX SUMMARY
Points to Remember

1) Effective leaders are unique. Being dele-gated the role of leader **does not neces-sarily qualify you as an effective leader**.

2) Effectiveness **is a constant process of multiplying** what works and eliminating what does not.

3) Effectiveness **is the only true measure** of leadership quality.

4) The effective leader **practices** research-proven qualities of effective leadership.

5) **Pattern your leadership development process** by the six qualities of an effective leader.

6) The real **servant leader** is the Developer — the effective leader.

Chapter Seven

Effective leadership is the key to over-coming organizational apathy!

Effective Leadership and the Organization

Now that you have reached the last chapter of this book, you may have some obvious questions, such as:

> **Can effective leaders really make that much of a difference?**
>
> **Why do I need to be concerned about effective leaders?**
>
> **My company is doing okay. Why can't we just hire or promote leaders and let them learn on the job? That is the way I did it.**

These are not fabricated questions. They are actual questions that I have been asked over the years. I usually reply with this metaphoric question:

> **Fresh paint sometimes looks good on a metal surface without a primer coat, so why waste your time with a primer coat?**

The subtle message of this question offers a hint of the common-sense answer to the above questions about effective leadership. A primer coat of paint takes *time*, *investment*, and *work*, but it protects the finish coat from rust over the long term. *The organizational focus on effective leadership at every level of the organization is the key to the excellence and sustainability of the organization.*

95

Why Excellence? Why Sustainability?

From a shallow perspective, excellence and sustainability *may not appear to be essential*. Many organizations simply get lost in the operational part of doing business and produce adequate results.

However, successfully moving an organization to the next level is difficult, *if not impossible*, without these two driving forces of excellence and sustainability.

> **Are excellence and sustainability essential if the business produces adequate results?**

If excellence and sustainability represent the *wheel* of the effective organization, effective leadership is the *hub* of that wheel.

What are excellence and sustainability?

Excellence is:

> **the passionate pursuit of a better tomorrow,**

> **the passionate spirit of excellence that raises continuous improvement to a higher level,**

> **the difference between an organization influenced by effective leaders and an organization that survives with leadership by promotion.**

Sustainability is:

> **the survival and growth of the quality of the organization despite the inevitable competition, economic upheavals, and uncontrollable circumstances that the future may hold,**

the primer coat of paint under a finish coat on a metal surface that perpetuates the finish coat.

There Is No Such Thing as a Natural Leader

I want you to eliminate for a moment the mental picture of the natural-born, charismatic leader.

Why? **Because effective leaders are developed, not naturally born**.

In fact the word "natural" **does not describe** the effective leader.

For example, take what you have learned from the contents of this book and apply it to the leaders you have experienced in your past or current situation.

It is unfortunate, but not surprising, that some readers may have never observed an effective leader.

The research from Jay Hall's *The Achieving Manager* study showed that effective leaders represent **approximately 14% of the leadership ranks**.

Highly effective leaders are rare!

Effective leaders at every level of the organization will do the following:

1) **foster** positive and creative work environments,

2) **deliver** measurable and sustainable results, and

3) **maintain** the ethical integrity of the workplace.

A brief discussion of the positive impact each of these contributions have on the organization may be helpful.

#1 — Foster Positive & Creative Work Environments

Positive and creative work environments usually describe an effective, corporate culture.

My definition of organizational culture is this:

> **A measure of the positive or negative quality of interpersonal support, communications, values, ideologies, behaviors, and relationships that exist within the organization.**

On a scale of 1 to 10, with 1 being the lowest and 10 being the highest, I have observed organizations with almost a perfect 10 in culture ... *and I have observed many organizations with barely a 1!*

Of course this is only a subjective measure, but you need only to experience it to actually *feel the tension and pressure* within an organization that has a low culture rating versus the high expectancy and passion of an organization with a high culture rating.

> **Sustainability is the survival and growth of the quality of the organization DESPITE the inevitable competition, economic upheavals, and uncontrollable circumstances that the future may hold.**

That is because *organizations with a high quality of culture are usually led by effective leaders.*

Another measure of a positive work environment is the measure of climate. Organizational climate is a measure of the **degree of positive or negative energy, attitudes, spirit, synergy, and team work that exists within an organization**.

Do not confuse climate with culture. They are not the same, though they are interrelated — one fosters the other.

What is culture?

> **It is a measure of the quality of interpersonal organizational support.**

What is climate?

> **It is a measure of the degree of energy and spirit.**

When I observe an organization with a high-quality culture and a high-energy climate, I **_always_** find effective leaders at the helm.

In these high-quality and high-energy organizations I also find a vital resource: **creativity!**

However, creativity is not always recognized by leaders as a resource. I have worked within some organizations that actually discourage it.

The organizations whose leaders consider creativity as a

> **Organizations with a high-quality culture and a high-energy climate ... always have effective leaders at the helm.**

process **exclusive to top leadership** unknowingly deprive themselves of a vital resource.

99

Effective leaders, on the other hand, foster creative work environments *because they develop collaborative opportunities to involve everyone in the thinking process of the organization.*

When leaders gain access to the individual thoughts and ideas of those who make up the organization, a higher level of thinking and collaboration is reached from which creativity and commitment are spawned.

Effective leaders see organizational creativity as a vital resource.

#2 — Deliver Measurable & Sustainable Results

Effective leaders not only foster positive and creative work environments, but also they deliver measurable and sustainable results.

Results management is the cornerstone of effective leadership. Effectiveness is the *only true measure of action*, and effective leaders consistently choose effective actions supported by measurable results.

Effective leaders deliver measurable and sustainable results because they are consistently driven by the process of

multiplying what works,

abandoning what does not, and

consistently measuring results, so they will always know the difference.

#3 — Maintain the Ethical Integrity of the Workplace

Finally, effective leaders maintain the ethical integrity of the workplace. They know that the long-term sustainability of an organization is dependent upon the ethical integrity of its leadership.

Effective leaders maintain the ethical integrity of the workplace *by consistently avoiding the comfort zone of self-centeredness*.

Their first consideration is others.

They know that the sustainability of the organization is in jeopardy *any time manipulation and deceit are tolerated*.

> **Organizations with a culture and climate of mistrust ... do not have effective leaders at the top.**

I have observed organizations that actually encourage their employees to come up with new and innovative ways to deceive the customer.

It will not surprise you to hear:

> **Such organizations are usually fraught with mistrust.**

Honestly, if employees observe intentional deceit from the leadership, how can they possibly trust the leadership with their best interests?

The result is an organizational culture and climate of mistrust, and I never find effective leaders in this type of environment.

101

Learn to Become an Effective Leader

In his book *The Leader of the Future*, the late Peter Drucker wrote:

> **"There may be 'born leaders' but there surely are far too few to depend on them. Leadership must be learned and can be learned."**

The validated research from *The Achieving Manager* study proves that the effective leader is the **Developer**. This effective model of leadership can be *learned* through a process that requires the development of consistent behaviors and beliefs rather than just the acquisition of knowledge.

Creativity is a resource.

Those organizations that heed the call of *building a culture of excellence and sustainability* must invest in the development of existing and future leaders.

In addition preliminary research demonstrates that effective leadership development enhances organizational climate and employee satisfaction ... *and there are indications that employee satisfaction may directly correlate with profitability!* Leadership development is not a cost at all but rather an investment with measurable return.

Leadership Development Is Top Priority

Every organizational leader should view the culture and climate of the organization as a top priority.

Productive culture and *passionate climate* are the byproducts of effective leadership.

In his book *Good to Great*, Jim Collins reported his research of certain companies that had made the transition from being a good company to becoming a great company. In every one of his successful examples, Collins found the common denominator was:

effective leadership.

You may be an aspiring leader, a seasoned veteran leader, or some-where in-between — it makes no difference.

The ideal of the perfect leader is a myth.

> **Real change and improvement is neither easy nor comfortable because potential always lies just beyond your comfort zone.**

As a leader you must choose the appropriate, effective actions to continue to grow regardless of your level of tenure or degree of success. There are no in-between positions in life where growth is no longer necessary.

You are now aware of the forces of apathy as a natural, human instinct.

You are now aware of your inherent, creative, personal powers to counteract the natural forces of apathy.

You are now aware of the qualities of the effective leader.

You are now aware of the significant impact of effective leadership within the organization.

Real change and improvement is neither easy nor comfortable because potential always lies just beyond your comfort zone.

However, real change

 begins with awareness, and

  awareness always leads to choice.

The real question you must ask yourself is this:

 How will I choose?

CHAPTER SEVEN SUMMARY
Points to Remember

1) Effective leadership at every level of the organization **is the key** to the excellence and sustainability of the organization.

2) Excellence is simply the **passionate pursuit of a better tomorrow**. It is the passionate spirit of excellence that raises continuous improvement to a higher level.

3) Sustainability **is the survival** and **growth** of the quality of the organization **regardless** of the inevitable, uncontrollable circumstances of operations over the long-term.

4) Highly effective leaders **are rare**. Research shows that effective leaders represent approximately 14% of the leadership ranks.

5) Effective leaders at every level of the organization **foster positive and creative work** environments, **deliver measurable** and sustainable results, and **maintain** the ethical integrity of the workplace.

6) Those organizations that heed the call of building a culture of excellence and sustainability **must invest in the development of existing and future leaders**.

7) Leadership development **is not a cost at all but rather an investment with measurable return**.

Epilogue

Effective leaders avoid the tripping point of apathy!

It Is Your Choice Now

If your choice is to become a more effective leader, I have written this epilogue for you.

Since the purpose of this book is to serve as a wake-up call for existing and future leaders, after finishing this book you may be asking the following questions:

Where do I go from here?

What steps can I take to learn about becoming a more effective leader?

There are many companies and individual consultants in the leadership development industry. You only need to go to your computer and do a search to find them. Some of those companies do a fine job with development.

> **Developing your untapped potential is not comfortable, but it is necessary in becoming an effective leader.**

There are many companies, however, promoting *training* and calling it *development*. Training is always appropriate when knowledge or new information is to be communicated.

However, there is a significant difference between training and development. For example:

Training is an event, but development is a process.

Training has little, if any, impact on behaviors that have been developed over a lifetime.

Leadership development involves much more than knowledge — it involves basic values, beliefs, and behaviors.

Behavioral change only comes from a development process. The best way to sift through the "noise" in this industry is to ask those companies a few questions regarding leadership development:

1) Do you use a development process?

2) Do you measure results?

3) Have you been in business for at least 10 years?

4) May I see a sample list of your clients by industry?

5) May I see a few sample case studies of successful engagements?

6) Is your process based on validated research?

7) Do you guarantee measurable results?

If you cannot get a **YES** to all of these questions, <u>**move on**</u> to the next option!

When you choose to become a more effective leader, *you must act on that choice.*

Yes, it will take time to become an effective leader.

Yes, it will cost money in the process.

Yes, it will take hard work.

But if you want to be something tomorrow that you are not today, it requires the development of your untapped potential.

It also requires that you counterbalance all apathy in yourself, your peers, and your organization.

Applying the "process" in this book is not comfortable, but it is necessary in becoming an effective leader.

I wish you Godspeed in your quest for effective leadership.

To communicate personally with David Byrd, call his offices at: 254-732-5493.

About the Author

David Byrd

David Byrd is a business leader, best-selling author, and dynamic keynote speaker. He has over 30 years of experience working with top leaders and their organizations, including serving as president of Leadership Management®, Inc., an international leadership and organizational development company.

David uses a development model that focuses on leadership development and organizational planning.

He completed both his undergraduate and graduate work at the University of South Carolina in 1969. He began his career as a high school football coach and later went on to coach at the college level. He began his career with LMI in 1979 as an LMI Partner in South Carolina. He was invited to join the LMI home office executive staff in 1981 and relocated to Waco, Texas.

David credits Paul J. Meyer, the founder of LMI, as being a significant influence in his work in the leadership development field and recognizes that everything in this book was stimulated from that influence.

He is very active in his church, First United Methodist Church of Waco, Texas, where he has served as an adult Sunday school teacher for over 20 years. His first book *Lessons for a Lifetime* is a summary of his experiences as an adult Sunday school teacher. David and his wife Mary have two daughters and five grandchildren.

You may contact David at
davidbyrd@trippingpointbooks.com

CONTACT THE AUTHOR

You can reach David Byrd,
master of effective leadership,
by calling:
254-732-5493
or emailing:
davidbyrd@trippingpointbooks.com

Apathy is a natural, human instinct,
common to us all, that consistently
encourages us to seek a comfort zone in
which nothing ever changes.

Now you know what to do about it!